the banal mumblings of an unremarkable yet likeable oaf

Enjoy my banal
mumblings
Col

colin anderson

Introduction

Memories…I have mine, some of the poems in here have been composed about events from the past (distant or not.) I am older now - borderline dead if you ask my daughter. If you were at any of these events, then the truth of what happened is probably somewhere in between what you think and what I think. The memories have had the time between happening and leaking out of my pen to evolve. At no point will I lie, I may have the details wrong, but those details are true to me.

What I do know is that all the emotions in here are very true. Whether celebratory, loving or downright seething with rage - I often write when fueled by more severe bouts of emotion. Many of these have been written in various coffee shops, sometimes about the people sitting close to me doing something that annoys, entertains or distracts me. Working on the presumption that I am perfectly normal and everyone else is weird, this might make sense. When you read this you may imagine me as the grumpiest of cynics, I am really not. I mean, I have my moments like the rest of us, but I don't think I would want to read a collection of poems that just said everything is groovy.

A lot of the poems are also inspired by either family or friends, I mean who else can drive you to the more extreme side of emotions. My family, like most in the world, are equally typical and atypical at the same time. We have our foibles, our talents, our difficulties, we annoy each other, we laugh at each other, we laugh with each other and above all else, we love each other. This book differs from my first book, it is more light-hearted and not a narrative. Read it however you like.

The purists out there may get annoyed that I am not following specific poetry rules, for that I am not sorry. I've never been one for rules, until it comes to having all of my CDs into alphabetical order by artist and then by title within artist. Alas, you may have gathered I am not classically trained. Many would go as far as saying I am not a proper poet.

'He's Not A Proper Poet'

No stanzas formed
Or couplets rhymed
Definitely no haiku

No sonnets to be found
Nor acrostic rhymes
Whenever he writes something new

He blags his way
From ode to ode
Wondering what to do

Definitely no prose
Just anything goes
By the seat of his pants he flew

I hope you enjoy some of my banal mumblings.

Dedicated to Penny and all the oafs out there,
especially the two that are my offspring.

the banal mumblings of an unremarkable yet likeable oaf

Middle aged scrabble

Not the board game you enjoy
Not the board game that allows you to play xi and smugly score 64

The unintended brain scrabble

The unintended brain scrabble that makes the disgraced
Canadian sprinter Ben Jackson
That makes the red and white mushroom a fly patharic
That spikey flower you like becomes an aga-thingy-mi-jig

The once honed brain that could list the middle names of the
1986 FA cup winning team?
Well now it swaps your daughters and wife's names up in your
head

The once sharpened brain that knew all the trigonometric values
within a quarter of a second?
Well now, it takes a five second defog to recall a 4 digit PIN

The razor-like brain that knew the binding energies of the first
92 elements to 4 significant places?
Now wonders what it went into the utility room for

Yet it can still recall lyrics for songs from over 50 years ago
It immediately starts singing another song as one finishes –
because of the mix tape it listened to in 1987
It can sing all the way through a song after hearing a one second
beat the intro (it'll just now say it was Robert Jones from the
Cult singing)

Brain clarity fades like eyesight
Yet readers are easily bought to resolve the issues of the eyes
If only the misted brain could remember where they last put the
glasses down...

How many plates

Quick!

The kids!

Get them to school
To band
To cricket
To basketball
To drama, to singing, to music, to circus bloody school and to swimming!
Just get them somewhere!

Spin those plates, don't let them drop…
Now add work
Which job? Why do I have 3!?
Where are you this week?
What day are you in London?
Birmingham? For how long?
What day?!
Who's taking? Who's picking up? Have you booked after school club? Breakfast club?
Did I book afterschool club already?
Do they do overnight stays in primary schools? Why not?!

Get these plates spinning
Don't forget the others
Is that one starting to wobble?

The kids!
Who's picking them up?
From where?
Who else are we picking up?
I have checked the bloody calendar!

Keep them all spinning…

Let's have a plate labelled parents
And another for a social life
I know we're knackered but we deserve one
A plate for yours, a plate for mine and the all important joint one

That one is about to fall!!! Get to it! Run! Quicker!!!

It's no wonder we sometimes break
It's no wonder we sometimes feel like sitting on the floor and
letting the whole lot come
crashing down like a cartoon Greek wedding

It's no wonder we neglect some plates

The you plate
The me plate
The us plate

That basketball

I saw you out of the corner of my eye as I was paying
You were, as ever, amazed by the large basket full of balls
The one you could spend hours at

Basketballs, footballs, volleyballs…
Different sizes
Different colours
Different bounciness
Different textures
What more could a 5 year old Toby want?

Then, then you find a Toby size basketball
Squeeze It
Hold it
In one hand
The other
Then both
Throw it and catch it
Bounce it
Your eyes light up
Then a look of concern erodes the initial glee
It's perfect

Then one, two, three fingers…three pounds
I watch your face as you work out the price

Times had been hard for a while
We thought you hadn't noticed

'Do you think Father Christmas could afford one of these?'

A bittersweet explosion
Pride and self-loathing surge through my veins
I vow that things are going to change, for the better, as we leave
hand in hand

You are dreaming about whether it might be in your stocking on
the soon to be here Christmas day

A 5 year olds eternity later, you are unwrapping

Excited, wearing my big woolly hat
In awe of all the presents
You unwrap each one carefully
You always did

You've seen the round one
Yet you avoid it
Maybe scared in case it is the wrong one

Eventually, carefully removing the pieces of tape
Your whole body lights with a glow that illuminates the whole
world
I promise you things will get better

Confusion squared

My arse is not sparse
Most rumps are quite plump

One's buttocks outline is curved by a design well founded
I'm never astounded how they are all quite so rounded

So why in a hotel do they do it?
Why do they think that we'll fit?

A babies bum fits perfectly on a rounded potty
An adult posterior has no straight lines on their botty

Hotels - I really can't fathom or fangle
Why you think a toilet should be a rectangle?

I've never seen a square derriere.

I will never get this...

Doctors waiting room

Ninety percent
Silent

Not a word
Stare blankly forwards
Avoiding eye contact with the skill of a southerner on the
London underground

The other ten percent
Happy to share out loud their symptoms in the mausoleum like
waiting room
To anyone
And everyone

An arthritic hip to a perforated womb
They don't care, they'll tell the whole room

Detailed description of prolapsed piles
Photos available on publicly shared files

The other ninety percent squirm in their seats
Praying for their name to be called

A pointless appraisal

Welcome to your appraisal! Lots of truths to be learned
All of our feedback is honest, no stones left unturned

That's amazing - I'm so glad to hear
I've really enjoyed my first half year

You've been absolutely fantastic, a real plus
We don't know how we coped before you joined us

That's nice of you to say
Now what can I do to improve day to day?

You have been so fantastic, it is hard to tell
We've been amazed how you fitted in so well

That's great - thanks again
But what can I do to improve my game?

We couldn't have asked for more
Honestly, you've performed without flaw.

Excellent, now this constructive feedback?
What are the areas in which I lack?

Improve!? Why just be who you are...
You'll continue to be our rising star

Amazing, more vague positives to take
Now what should I work on? What changes should I make?

We have covered so much ground today.
Delved into the tough areas I'd say!

Can we at least set some targets before I leave?
Something tangible and quantifiable to achieve?

It's been such a constructive meeting since you came through that door
See you in 6 months, we can challenge you once more…

sighs

*Dedicated to Ged, my spoon playing friend, after he rang up ranting having just sat in his first appraisal that went exactly along those lines

I'm incapacitated

There's a friend who I call quite often
He's busy - can't always accept the call
'I'm in a meeting' comes the automated text reply
Not a problem as I'm generally moaning about not much at all

Today? His response, it was different
He responded in an alternative way
'I'm incapacitated' the text said this time
Just what was he trying to say?

He could have replied as normal
Why did he message something new?
My grey cells sparked for a moment
Until I realised he was having a poo

*Names have not been added to protect the person, but I'd like to thank Carl Turner for the inspiration.

Pebble

The summer holidays were not going smoothly for you
Although only 4 or 5, life seemed to be insurmountable
A challenge you were not relishing
I was the target of your frustrations

On a pebble beach, you walked away
Searched diligently for what seemed like a lifetime
With a focus I'd not seen in you before

Pick one up
Inspect
Put it down
Repeat

Until eventually one ticked all the boxes
You walked back to me
Placed it in my hand and walked away without a word

That pebble is with me always
Declining in size but growing in importance
As you grow and I decline

And the cups go in that one

Above the conveyor belt there were three holes

On labelled Plates
The next, Bowls
The final one, Cups

At a factory outside of Sydney Kingsford Smith Airport, a shiny, enthusiastic supervisor explains

'When the clean stuff comes out, you put plates in that hole'
gesturing towards the hole marked plates
Similar for the bowls before I boldly interrupted

'And the cups going there, right?'

His surprise was visible as he nodded with pride. Patting himself on the back because his teaching was obviously improving

Forty minutes or sixteen years later (I am unsure which) I knew I recognised the man at the next conveyor belt.

'If you don't guess by lunch I'll tell you then' he yelled over the intense white noise

Two centuries later at lunch, I sat with Grange Hill's very own prankster Gonch Gardner in a canteen full of automaton/people hybrids.

Trays back on the rack
'Are you ready? The buzzer is about to go' asks John

'Nope' I reply as I head for the door, lanyard in hand

The first day off

Yes,
Yes you can just sit there.

No,
No you don't have to do something.

Yes,
Yes I know your mind is racing.

No,
No you don't need to justify sitting down.

Yes,
Yes it's fine - but first I might just…

The Line

I understand
Sometimes it's far away
Sometimes almost tangible

For years it was invisible to me
Even though I unknowingly skirted very close
But now? I know it's there

It's a line I have no desire to cross
Its a line we're all aware of
It's a decision we have all contemplated, even if just for a
moment when near the edge of the precipice

My journey so far means I comprehend why other people
crossed it
I can empathise
My relationship with the line now is healthy

We're happy for society to be aware
When a stranger talks or listens we applaud them
Grateful times have changed

But for loved ones
We don't want to hear it
Through fear of where it oft ends

Crockashitzapoo

We've bought it lots of cutesy dressing up suits
So he doesn't get tired, we'll carry him all over
To save his little paws, we even bought some boots
He needs a funky little modern name, definitely not a Rover

She's a cocker-mocha-pocker-poo
She only cost us 14 grand
Don't mention to us rescue dogs, that subject is taboo
I'll make up twenty bullshit reasons and dismiss it out of hand

Ten years ago, a labra-doodle didn't exist
Back then it was just a mongrel, didn't need a fancy name
You keep on supporting the horrific puppy farms with their ever increasing price list
Yet everyone is certain theirs is from a reputable breeder - and they're sticking to that claim

Rescue centres across the country are full to overflowing
A cost of living crisis merely adding more trouble to the pan
Across the land, foodbank numbers are evergrowing
But you justified 5k for your dog because it is half husky half doberman

No matter how much you justify it, I'll never understand you
The misguided ethics you seem to have don't trouble you one bit
If someone were to breed a Jack Russel and a Shitzu
It would equal your excuses, they both add up to JackShit

It's my fault really

It's not your fault
I know you're lonely
I know you appreciate the company
The conversation
The consistency
And the familiarity

But I have one hour
One hour of peace
To read my book
Drink my drink
And let my brain slow down

It's not your fault
It's not your fault that you have an omnipresent droning voice
that permeates and penetrates every single nook and every single
cranny of the cafe I am trying to relax in

It's not your fault that in your desire to converse you are willing
to incessantly make noise by stringing what seems like any
combination of words together
Talk about anything
Absolutely anything
Constantly

It's my fault
I should be more patient
I should empathise more
But I only have an hour
So please
At least for ten minutes
Shut up
So I can write a poem

Alpaca defence

I stand here before you Judge
Ready to clear my name
As an alpaca, this is really quite a privilege
To get a chance to fully defame

Even as an animal, it really made me blush
He took me for a walk, held me my bit
Everything was normal, until he took me behind the bush
When he pulled his pants down and quickly did a shit

"It wasn't my shit, it was Alpaca shit" I heard him shout
So here I am in front of you to clear my reputation
Dear judge I am innocent, I want you to have no doubt
I'd like to start my case now, one I call the Defecation
Defamation.

Entities in a family fridge

A family fridge has a lot to put up with
The treats and the delights
The half bottle of wine and other such staples
Then occasionally some things that may have developed into new
medical discoveries

The busiest place of all is the condiment shelf
All desperate to be picked
Do they jostle at night to get to the front?
The weakest, the organic miso, whimpers meekly at the back
Knowing it's only hope of beating its use by date is for someone
to choose a Japanese night

The left-over shelf
A layer full of good intentions
But everyone knows you should have put it in the freezer
Instead, too many days later it looks like a cross between Louis
Pasteur's work and a Jackson Pollock.

But then, skulking in the tray at the bottom
Shielded by the veg and the salad
Lurking with intention and trying not to look like some random
bits of nature
Waiting patiently for their starring role as the baddies in the new
spiderman film
The Rancid Pineapple and the Unintended Kombucha…

Unintended Kombucha

Leftovers hidden
Await the fridge opening
Fermented surprise

Fresh ground snobbery

A gorilla and a cactus
A supernova and a pantomime dame
Can all be linked if you try hard enough
But you wouldn't say they're the same

When someone reaches for a jar of instant coffee
Far fetched relationships spring to mind
I'd approximate Nescafè more to Bisto
Before I'd assimilate it with a fresh coffee bean grind

Chickens are closer to dinosaurs
Than an espresso is to GoldBlend
So please don't offer me one of yours
As refusal can sometimes offend

Addicted? Moi?

I'm definitely not addicted
It's 10am, I've just snarled and called my car keys a twat

Signals recognised
Double espresso en route

Aaaannnnd relax, the world is fine
OK, maybe I am slightly addicted

We all need our vices

Tut and sigh combo

Middle class middle aged tutting
Two people at one point exchanged glances
Raising eyebrows with a jovial tut and a smile

The Barbour clad lady gave a faultless tut and head-shake combo
Sent a shiver down the spine

You can't pay or weigh loose fruit and veg
Enough to send some people over the edge

One lady, enraged, stormed off with a huff
Sacrificing her kale smoothie and ripen-at-home avocado
Replaced perfectly back onto the correct shelf of course
Labels facing forwards, she's not an animal

The chap behind her contemplated it
But the thought of an evening without haloumi and quinoa give
him the courage to try
So he gave a winning tut, sigh and head shake to the sky

Blitz spirit at it's finest
We're all in this together
We can make it

This is not just any till breakdown
This is an M&S till breakdown

Hold that phone

Does the side of your head not work?
For the first 20 years of mobiles it was clear
You could simply hold the phone to your ear

Could it be a matter of health?
Is it to protect you from the rays from space?
Is that why you hold it in front of your face?

Is it the fault of Lord Sugar?
A sign of importance to hold out front and flat?
Are you a 'someone' if you hold it out front like that?

Do you not want to keep your chat private?
Because believe it or not as I sit here in this cafe
I have absolutely no urge to know what you have to say

When are 'they' going to do something about it?

Although I don't know who **they** may be
They best hurry up and do something about it
So long as it doesn't inconvenience me
I shouldn't have to alter my life, not one little bit

I should be free to do as I please
Concrete pattern drive and some astro turf?
Turn the heating on full or the aircon to freeze
It's really not my fault if it's costing the earth

Because they just need to come up with a plan
One that means I can keep buying all my fast fashion
It's definitely not the fault of the common man

A few burning chimps? Why should I show compassion?

There's one main thing they need to remember
This thing is cyclic, happens all the time
Just a coincidence It's 40 degrees in December
I know I'm right…

       hold on, was that the doomsday clock I just heard chime?

The perfect companion?

The grey haired terrier that fits perfectly under your table in
your local
The cat that'll be stroked forever
The sketchbook that never refuses your drawings
The dog-eared book you've read over and over and over
The point and shoot camera that'll always take the shot
The sleeping baby in the pushchair that listens to all you have to
say
The houseplants that pay attention as they're sprayed, clipped
and dusted
The path up the hill that leads to the view you'll never get bored of
The album that can deal with any mood you throw at it
The bench that is perfectly placed on your walk so your flask of
tea is just at the right temperature
The person that listens to that anecdote for the umpteenth time,
and they still smile at the punchline

Is it possible to have just one perfect companion?

First game for the firsts

I don't need you to be the hero
Take a five-fer and knock a quick fifty
I don't need you to take the catch that wins the cup
For your sake
For my sake
Just don't fuck it up

Waiting on a deckchair

An hour
Sixty whole minutes
Three thousand six hundred seconds

To do nothing…But wait

Normally a beautiful experience

But not this time

This time I sat on a deckchair
It looked inviting, it was just there

Now I've sat on it, I feel I should give it a while
The memories of deckchairs full of nostalgia and old holiday
style

The truth is I don't fit anymore

I'm too long, too broad, I don't fit inside
My arse doesn't fit and my shoulders too wide
58 minutes to go…

Handcuff accents

Why does our tonality mean people decide who we are?
Pronunciation can make sure doors are never ajar

How dare you not be an ex-Eton country gent
We'll invisibly imprison you with your handcuff accent

Whereas if you enunciate a we say it should be
Then we'll give you a universal skeleton key

It'll open all those doors that to others remain shut
Only they know the secret as to where they are cut

Glass ceilings are invisible, hard to get through
But not if you have the decency to speak as we do

Now the tide, it is turning, at a slow snails pace
Two hundred years in, both still in the race

The youth and disruptors don't care if they fit
Because times? They are a changin', innit

Five star check-in

Ah Sir, I see you are wearing worker type clothes
You know we can't trust you, that, everybody knows

Now you want to check into our beautiful five star resort
Although having guests like you is a habit we really should abort

Your attire tells us that you are intellectually challenged, to you
that means thick
Not like the gent in the corduroy, doesn't he look slick?

Your uniform says such an awful lot about you
You're undignified, inelegant and hence you are now at the back
of my queue

If only you had the decency to sport a nice tie
The reasons are too complex for you to understand why

You can just take a seat over there whilst we metaphorically pat
you on the head and wonderfully patronise
Whilst we help this lady in the suit, but please don't be visible,
we don't want to stain her eyes.

So long as you know you're not one of our kind
And next time you're booking, please don't bear us in mind

*One of my jobs has me wearing work clothes, the change in attitude
towards me is phenomenal.*

Bland hotel in Swindon

There he sits
In a bland hotel in Swindon
That weird bloke in the corner

Reading a book
Which is almost a crime in itself

But then he goes one step further
Takes it quite frankly beyond the pail

He laughs

Not just a chuckle
Not just a snigger
But a full on laugh
A proper laugh with a 'haha' sound that breaks the bland
silence draped over the bland lounge, enforced by bland silence
enforcing guards

'How dare he?' - the eyes of three headed 6 tentacled cyborg
salesman say whilst he is trying not to drown in his own drool

'Despicable' thinks the lady who has been sat here so long she
has morphed into a stripy bucket chair and can no longer leave as
she can't fit out of the door

Whilst one rebel in the corner who has only been imprisoned
for 3 months looks longingly thinking the weirdo may be his own
Blake 7 style saviour.

The weirdo then picks up his pen and writes a poem before
buying a pint and taking it outside

The stripy sofa woman weeps into the stripy carpet and whispers
'bastard'

*I apologise to Swindon, I have no idea if you are bland or not, it just happened
to be my location when I had a few hours alone in the bar.

Teenagers at Christmas

October: Very organised
What do you want for Christmas?
I don't know, it's October…

Early November: Hoping for a hint?
What do you want for Christmas?
Dunno, not thought about it…

Late November: Surely an idea?
What do you want for Christmas?
I don't know, just money, stop asking…

Early December: Perhaps one big thing?
What do you want for Christmas?
Leave me alone, just money…

Mid December: Maybe a few little things?
What do you want for Christmas?
I don't know!!! Just socks or something…

December 22nd: Too late now.
I've had a thought about what I want for Christmas.
I'd like
This sports kit
These shoes
That game we played on holiday
That jacket we saw in August
This music
That ticket
That book
This computer game
These earphones
This microphone
These trainers…

My tulips and honesty

My tulips and honesty are rather complimentary
Can't say the same about my daffs, they're always rude to me

He's a plasterer

He's a plasterer, always in demand
I swear he was born with a hawk in his hand

Being a spread kept him fit and healthy
Shame it didn't keep him rich and wealthy

Ladders needed to overcome his short demeanour
As messy as he is short, he could be a bit cleaner

Alas now he's getting on, his trowel, it sees less action
Now he seems to just drive his beloved wife to distraction

When he eventually slips off this mortal coil
And before we stick him in a box and cover it in soil

We should slip in his handboard and trowel whilst the funeral car
awaits
In case St Peter needs him to render the walls by the pearly gates

No shite on my salad

Salad on the side
Please
Just leave it be

No salad dressing, no mayonnaise
No lemon and mustard vinagrette
Nor any balsamic glaze

Just leave it be
Put the dressing on the side
Then how much and where is up to me

I'll have as much as I want
Where I want
When I want
How I want

If I want

Thank you, that has surely covered all possible smearing,
dressings and oilings*

*side salad arrives covered in coleslaw

Portmanteaus galore

Very often they work, they help you anoint
Increase the succinctness of your point

When hunter gatherers did their thing
Why can't we say they're going huntering?

The contented warmth of finishing a good read
Call that satisfiction, why not indeed?

The feeling of hanger in our house we know well
Both me and my daughter can create a peckish lead hell

To chortle comes from a chuckle and a snort
A word we all use without a thought

Social media throw out new ones at a pace
Slacktivists and Frenemies all over the place

As always there are places we really shouldn't go
Some people create a portmanteau no-no

A Boobgasm was once used on a Cosmopolitan front page
Came and went quickly, didn't really age

You do have to wonder who came up with that
And if their editor called them a compwat

Fast Fashion

"It keeps **them** in a job" goes the platitude
The reality for **them** is more one of servitude

Primark, H&M, George and the rest
Just a profit is needed to pass their moral test

For some, who seldom have a voice
The costs of life give them little or no choice

For most it's fast fashion and nothing but greed
The desire to have what you want and not what you need

I'll pick what I want and take it home today
But won't want it tomorrow and throw it away

Fast fashion costs so much more than what it says on the tag
A price you don't see when carrying a fully laden bag

The chemicals, the pollution, the plastic, the enslavement
But don't let that cloud your mind as you pound the pavement

Millions of unwanted tonnes dumped in the Atacama
Like the sick made-up dream of a dystopian farmer

But it's OK, you've got a new top for tonight
It does keep them in a job, enslaved to their predestined plight

Inspirational Quotations

They can appear everywhere
Twee tea towels
Faux aged signs
Tee shirts
Posters
Social media posts
Management books
Wherever you are, they are there
Ready to auto-impose their wisdom upon you

They can appear in of all those places and more
And unfortunately do
Forced messages trying to infiltrate my world
Patronising me on an industrial scale

Well I have my one too
Whenever I see or hear an inspirational quotation
I recall my own

'Stick it up your arse you sanctimonious git'

Now put that on your tea towel and get out of my face

Drive dreaming

Do you ever, when driving home, get the urge to turn left
instead of right?
And then just keep on going

One of those days when you could drive and drive
Stopping only to fill up the car before setting off again

Setting off on the road to…
The road to somewhere
You don't know where
Just somewhere

Somewhere that isn't here
Where you are meant to be

Driving away from where you are needed
The where in which you have to…
Pick the kids up
Put the washing away
Empty the dishwasher
Drop the kids off
Sort out the house insurance
Drop off somebody else's kid
Stick the dog in the washing machine and take the bedding for a
walk

You dream as you drive
The crisp, clear mountains
The big city lights
The rolling hillsides
The long stretching beaches
The eternal forests
The lakeside view
The possibilities are endless

That's where you're heading
They'll move on without you and you'll keep rolling
You'll be the enigmatic stranger that flits from place to place
Never laying down any roots
Nobody is going to tame the new you!

Then you park outside your house
Grab the shopping and go in

Disappearing sands

Time that I simply gave away
Time that I can never get back

I don't why I did it
It was just there
I touched the screen in a moment of madness whilst eating my
lunch

And nobody made me

Then I watched ten whole minutes
Six hundred of my precious seconds given to 'A Question of
Sport'

My time

Gone
Why?

We're parents, it's our job

As a parent, what is our main role?
To turn our kids into well rounded girls and boys?
To make sure when older they fulfil a goal?
Let's be honest, that is nothing but noise…

Because something happens as soon as your child is here
New parents all gather together in a special secret event
When you first get there you have no idea
Until they tell you that you must be an embarrassing parent…

When the car window is open you must sing at the top of your voice
Dance in the supermarket aisle - and tell your now hiding child 'I don't care!'
I don't care if they see me or hear me, I'm happy, that's my choice!
You don't think I'll go out wearing this pink fluffy hat? Is that a dare!?!

Because dear children - it is what we must do
It is the law, it's our role in this place
No need to be embarrassed by our flowery shoes
No need to hide or have a red face

So the next time a parent volunteers to get up on stage
Sings karaoke and really makes you want to hide
Remember that when you are of an older age
It will be your turn soon, be patient, abide

Wonky twange

It's Wonky and I don't know how to fix it
There's no wotsit to tighten or doodah to twist

The doctor said it was nothing to do with him
The mechanic she's de-wonked a few things, but not that

The optician said it was far too complicated
The engineer gave a gallic shrug and a Non

Just what can I do with my Wonky Twange?
The chiropractor wanted to crack it into place

The homeopath thought I was some kind of psychopath
The Chinese herbalist had no solutions as a solution

The wonk merely gave the acupuncturist the needle
The reiki master said it was too hot to handle

The jedi master? Not help with it, could they
Just what can I do with my Wonky Twange?

Perhaps…perhaps it's not wonky and it is really just right?
Perhaps it is perfect and it's us on the wonk?

Maybe, just maybe, all twanges are meant to be wonked…

If with this I am happy then a new problem arises
What do you do with a twange? Wonky or not

On the offer of a brew

You get offered a hot drink
'That'd be lovely, thanks'
Thumbs up in gratitude

Now asked if you want tea or coffee
This should be the easy part
Just pick one
Whichever one you most feel like
Just pick one and say it

Instead
'Whatever you're making' – I am only making one for you, tea or coffee?

'Whichever is closest to your hand' – They're both right in front of me, tea or coffee?

'Whichever is easiest' – I am an adult, perfectly capable of making both, tea or coffee?

'I'm not bothered, you choose' – No, that is why I asked you, you are going to drink it, please will you just choose whichever one you want, tea or coffee?

'So long as it is wet and warm' – They are both wet, they are both warm, for crying out loud will you just choose one. Either tea. Or coffee.

'Either one is good with me' – Maker sighs and puts both in a cup

Old fashioned Grandmother

Old boots? Bunch of wusses,
Not tough in the slightest

We've all had one
Still got one if you're lucky

That grandmother
She'd send Arnie back to his future with his tail between his legs
Sigourney's alien would clean up the mess from the giant gloopy
eggs and apologise
Krüger would stay in his basement

They single handedly held the family together every day
Cooking for any number
Clothing magicked up from somewhere
Keeping all in check whilst simultaneously maintaining the
home's spick and span rating high in case the lady from 2 doors
down popped in
Through war, famine and whatever else life would dare throw at
them

Apollo Creed would ask for forgiveness whilst wiping the sweat
he just dripped on the boxing ring floor
Godzilla would retreat quickly back into his ocean home
The Godfather would take the cotton wool out of his cheeks and
make her a cup of tea

They may have been small
They may have been poor
Life's luxuries may have passed them by
But as Springsteen said, they are definitely tougher than the rest

Like Rambo with pink toenails

Promises broken

It'll be different this time…
How am I supposed to believe you? You said that 3 weeks ago…

But this time I mean it, like really mean it…
The same words!!! You used exactly the same phrase 3 weeks ago and you still expect me to believe you now?

I know, I know but this time it is different, I don't know why but it just feels different…
You really do expect me to believe you don't you?!

I promise…
What exactly are you promising?

That I won't just chuck tools in at the end of the day…
Heard that before…

And when I am reaching for the tool that's gone slightly underneath another one, I won't just yank it so they all go everywhere…
And that

And that I'll put tools back in their correct places rather than just fill buckets with the tools I've been using that day
Hmmph

And, and, and, that I'll sweep you out once a week!!!
Yeah right, of course you will

One last chance?
Have I got any choice?

I guess not but it'll be different this time…
Chat to you in 3 weeks again then yes? So you can promise the same things again?

Probably, sorry…
Whatever.

(The landscaper and their van schedule another meeting for 3 weeks…)

Oxford scallops

We've all heard of Delhi Belly
But be careful down in Oxfordshire
I went down there to film some telly
And some scallops left me feeling rather dire

I'd had 14 pints of Bertie's Crapshifter Cider
A 16 percenter, full of straw and other bits
Made you feel like you had a farmyard inside yer
But there's no way on earth that the cider gave me the shits

Those pesky bloody scallop things
Messin' around in me tummy
Made sure I got the ring stings
And left me feeling rather funny

*Dedicated to Gruff, who, to this day, insists it was the scallops even though the rest of us ate them too.

On another note, if there is a cider manufacturer out there who wants to make some Bertie's Crapshifter, get in touch, I'll drink cider for the first time since I was 13.

Corridor greetings

You Ok?
Y'alright mate?
How's your week been?

All question greetings we ask
That in truth, we don't really mean

Don't honestly reply to those questions we proffer
We actually don't want to know
We haven't got time for the answer
We've somewhere that we need to go

You nod and smile and say that you're good
Before returning the question, after all, it's your turn to ask
Because it is fully expected, we say what we know that we should
But nobody really answers, we just say 'good' and keep on the mask

If someone didn't answer properly, we'd stop right there where
we were
Do we stay and give time to that person in need?
Or panic and scarper, with no time to care
Do we have the skills, or desire, to stop and take heed?

Snigwirting

In work I do tow things
I sell cofnectionary
Print tee shrits every day
One day I lost contencration
Because I ate so much fugde

Defecated to Paul Edmunds and the shop on Blackpool front

Solidified

Yer wot?
Wot did he say?

Chatting after school in group of some peers
When I made a statement that drew in the jeers

'In chemistry, instead of went 'ard - he said it solidified!'
'Ooooh' said the crowd as I tried to hide

How many years until I can be in a place
Where talking with syllables is not a disgrace?

I knew deep inside, they all had my back
But I just wasn't made for a world this full of flak

It's Mum's birthday, can I...

"Can I make Mum some brownies for her birthday?"
The cry comes from below

It'll be fun
It'll be good for them
It'll teach them so many good skills
What a lovely thoughtful child

Of course there are never enough things in the cupboard
Off to the supermarket we go

But not just any old supermarket
We have to go to the organic, vegan, bespoke, plastic free, locally
sourced, fair trade, rainforest alliance, dolphin friendly version

Forty five pounds later
We have 10 small irregular brownies

We also have a kitchen that looks like the Oompah Loompahs
went on a frenzied rampage after Willy Wonka summarily
dismissed them all due to a new 'no orange skin' rule.

One industrial clean later
Twenty three thousand five hundred and twenty eight
compliments about the brownies to the chef later

The mouth speaks again

"Can I make some bath bombs for Mum's birthday?"
Your wallet let's out an audible sob as you reply 'That's a lovely
idea, Mum will love that'

Our Carol's samosas

Our Carol makes me a cracking samosa
Makes them from scratch, a real culinary performer

But yesterday I bought some at my local deli
One of those posh delis you see on the telly

Eurgh, it was full of all kinds of veg and loads of spice
Not like Carol's, nowhere near as nice

Was it the fault of the spices and other such nasties?
Or has our Carol been calling them samosas instead of just
pasties?

*I will never know how the person behind the deli counter put up with
this woman complaining because the samosas she bought were samosas.*

I'm on the train

'Yes, sorry, my signal is rubbish. I'm on the train'

So why did you call?
Why has half the carriage called someone to tell them they're on
the train?
You know the signal will be bad
You know you'll get cut off
You know you'll have to repeat most sentences three times
Each time little louder as though that'll help strengthen the
signal
Your wry smile as you have to redial for the 4th time
Even though this is your commuter train and you know exactly
where you lose signal
Because yesterday,and the day before, and the day before…
You called a different friend and said

'Yes, sorry, my signal is rubbish. I'm on the train'

What a good little doggy you are...

Rover, Rover! Come back!
Don't worry, he's only playing,
He just gets excited
So sorry, it's only a little rip in your jeans.

Rover! Rover! I said come here,
Don't worry, he's only playing,
He gets nervous around other dogs,
So sorry, I'm sure the vet will sort it for you.

Rover! Rover!! Get off it,
Don't worry, he's only playing,
He must have smelt the food,
So sorry, the steak will be fine if you give it a wash.

Rover, ROVERRR!! Let go of her,
Don't worry, he's only playing,
He does give a little nip sometimes,
So sorry, would you like your fingers back?

Rover!!! ROVERRR!!! Come here boy,
Oh what a good little doggy you are...

Not today thank you

It can wait
Whatever it is
It can wait

Work, the dishes, that email, that drop off and pick up, whatever
it is
It can wait

Right here, right now
I'm rebelling
I'm calling it quits
I'm sticking it to the man
I'm changing the sign on the front door to closed
I'm switching off the lights and sitting on my arse
I'm having a duvet day
You, her, him, they, them
Can all sod off
Do one
Get out of my face

Because today, I just don't feel like it
I'm not taking part in the charade that my life sometimes is

*Sits for twenty seconds before switching the lights back on, turning the
sign to open, sighing and getting on with whatever was supposed to be
happening*

Nevermind, maybe next time…

Definitely not nervous

I got a phone call from school
Asking to collect you early

You definitely were <u>not</u> nervous

The headache, the funny tummy, the dizziness
All of them genuine illness

It was purely coincidental that you had your first stage
performance in 4 hours time
Pure, unadulterated coincidence

We got you home
On the sofa, under the duvet, hot water bottle and some calpol

I promise you, it's OK to be nervous, it's normal

Even though you are definitely not nervous

Definitely not

Slowly into costume, sipping your ginger tea
Eek slowly to the van
You get distracted by telling me of Lucy's run of bad luck for the
journey

Until
Until the carpark

'I don't want to'
'Don't make me go'
'What if I am sick on stage?'
'What if I mess it up for everyone?'
'Can we just go home?'

The illness still a coincidence

It's freezing so we need to cuddle all the way to the theatre

At the theatre, you see a fellow actor
Coolness kicks in
You head through the stage door with a nonchalant shrug

I return with the family two hours later
You pretend not to see us from the stage

The music gets louder
The lights dim
The audience stops chatting
Ebernezer Scrooge, sits up in his bed
We're off

Five minutes in
It's my turn to definitely not be nervous

I know you can do it
I really do know you can do it
I really want you to be amazing

You go to the back of the stage and enter the spotlight through
the door
The philanthropist asks Scrooge for a donation

You were word for word perfect
Showing fear for the now seething Ebernezer

You did it
You were amazing
You did it
My eyes well up
You did it

You did it

You see out the rest of the play
Take the applause at the finale

Then return to our fold
Two foot taller than you left us

You did it
You proved your amazingness
You did it*

*But you definitely were not nervous

Photos of loved ones

We carry photos of passed loved ones around
Memories of love that are forever bound
Some people wear them by their hearts in a locket
Others in a wallet in their jeans arse pocket

Punchbag

I rain down blow after blow after blow
A constant barrage of abuse
Emotional punch follows emotional punch
I boo the Duracell Bunny - no staying power

You're my punchbag
You'll never complain
No matter what I throw
You'll absorb it and move on

But nobody take my punchbag away
I'll hug you and kiss you and hug you some more
Long for you until you return
When I'll hug you and land a welcome back punch

How long will it be?
Before I see
How long will it be?
Before it dawns on me...

Once more unto the breach

They say nothing can truly prepare you for the horrors of war

Yet Baden Powell told us failing to prepare is preparing to fail

So here I am
Ready for battle
Equipment checked and double checked

The mind? As focused as it can be in the circumstances
Visualising all eventualities
Including the real risk of casualties
Hoping we all make it to the other side

One last breath before
Unto the breach we go my friends

Ready to help my child with their homework
May the force be with me

Peace

Table for one please
Double espresso arrives
Water on the side

The Premier Lodge Inn Travel Express

Welcome to the Premier Lodge Inn Travel Express
No, not the same, we're unique, different to the rest

As we give you our heartfelt, generic check-in schpiel
Remember to smile, no matter how you feel

We won't listen to the answer but 'have you stayed here before?'
Now we'll tell you bland information as you edge towards the
door

You will now receive our best plastic smile
Before you head down a corridor, for what feels like a mile

But I do have a question Mr Generic Hotel
Why stripey carpets? Why not rebel?

Your competitors all have them lining their floor
Do you all get a discount in the Stripeyland Superstore?

Return in the evening, What number's my room?!
Another bad night's sleep in your temporary tomb

Follow the stripes to make your egress,
Thank you for staying in the Premier Lodge Inn Travel Express.

Do one

You? You can just fucking do one
Get out of my fucking face
Whoever you are, just be gone
Disappear without a trace

Pontificating over Pontefract

Pontefract
Pontefract
Just listen to it
Say it
Repeat the name out loud
Look in the mirror
Emphasise the syllables
Then envisage it's beauty
In the heartland of Wales

Who put it in Yorkshire?

Then travel to another beautiful town

Languishing on the West Coast of Ireland

Which buffoon put Billericay in Essex?

It's like putting Loch MacTavish in Cornwall

False witness

Yes Officer, I saw it all from behind this wall
The solid one which is ten feet tall
I saw both of the trio attack
All four of them attacked the schoolboy from behind as the
victim looked them in the eye
The five of them just ran away laughing
Leaving her lying on the ground
What kind of a society do we live in?
When six people can attack an innocent pensioner...

A table for one please

Just you tonight?

The question, nay borderline accusation, that makes out
something is awry

Friends couldn't make it?
Spouse not like you?
Mistress couldn't get out?

Well I am sorry but you really don't get it

A table for one is a cause for celebration
It should be held in high esteem

Please don't judge, please don't assume

Two starters and 3 sides? Crack on
Wine and beer? Nobody to judge

Your choice to read, to watch, to listen or just to be…
To be in the moment
To sit
To contemplate
To stare vacantly into the distance enjoying an empty mind

I'll leave the table when I want
A purely selfish choice, not having to consider any other being

Billy Joel once referred to people sharing a drink called
loneliness but that is not always the case
Tonight Billy, you're wrong
I'm enjoying a drink I call peacefulness
Maybe I am big headed but I consider myself to be great
company

So, dear restaurateurs
Please don't ask if it is just for one
And please don't hide me in the corner next to the loos
I want pride of place in your restaurant
Somewhere I can see, be seen and just be the wonder that is me

I will sit, eat and drink whilst being wholly grateful that I am not
having to make small talk with a colleague

I might chill and read my book
Or maybe I'll write a poem

I want (Part 1)

For one night only
I want…

I want to not drive anyone to any club or sporting event
I want there to be no shoes scattered around the floor in random places
I want there to be no work email that just needs answering
I want the kitchen to be tidied by the cleaning fairy
I want there to be no mail on the to-be-sorted pile
I want there to be no washing in any of the baskets
I want everything to be in its place
I want to read my book
I want want my music to be playing
I want my sofa

I just want to be me with all the white noise taken away
Alas, maybe it'll happen once I've done the dishes, put this washing away, tidied the front room and sent that email…

I want (Part 2)

I want you to be your successful
To be happy and have enough friends

I want you to learn from your mistakes
And hold you hand up when you're wrong

I want you to never know true poverty
And appreciate all that you have

I want you to love, laugh and live
But don't ever have it written on a tea towel on your wall

I want you to take your old man for a pint
Even though he's a boring old fart

I want you to experience life at its best
Though I don't want to know all the details

Failing all of that
I want you to be just like that chicken

And get to the other side
I want you to know that I love you

*The two sides of parenting

Snooze or stop

Snooze or Stop
    A choice to be made
The temperature
The rain
The day that lies ahead
All have their opinions on which to choose

Snooze or Stop
    A choice to be made
Last night's red wine
The general chaos of life
The maniacal day that lies ahead
All opine as to which way you swipe

Snooze or Stop
    A choice to be made
Either up and at 'em as keen as can be
Or a temporary ceasefire before

Snooze or Stop
    A choice to be made

Waiting at a station for a friend

Where can I wait?
Where can I be so I am there but not there?

I don't want to look like a victim
Nor a soon-to-kill mass murderer.

Lean on the wall - away from the corner
Don't want to scare people as they come around

Try to look friendly - someone caught your eye
Not that friendly! They think you're one of those weird blokes

Not that dour either
Not like you want to disembowel them.

There's a seat at bus bay T
Good, sitting down
Inconspicuous - that's me

Shit, the bus is here
No thanks driver,
I don't want your bus
I'm just sitting here
Why? I'm waiting for a friend
Yes, I do have friends actually...

The easy way out

'They took the easy way out'

Words we have heard and will no doubt hear again
Generally by those whose egos outweigh their empathy

The strength of character you had is immense
You had a courage I hope I'll never know

To take those pills
To make that last step
To tie that rope

I just wish you'd called
I just wish you'd asked
I just wish you'd never found that strength at that time

I would have been there for you
You might still have been here for us

Parenting a pessimist

What if I don't like the sauce?
What if I hate it?
What if it rains?

You love that sauce, you equally might have the best time ever.
Who cares?! We've got coats…

What if there's no food left?
What if they had to close early today?
What if it is too hot?

It's a restaurant! Why would they have closed early just today?
Take that massive jumper off!

What if they closed early because it went on fire?
What if I don't like any people there?
What if they are all boooooooorrrrrrriiiiinnnnngggg?

It is by a lake! You may find a new best friend and have the best
time ever…

What if an alien eats you?
What if it explodes because a gorilla found a massive bomb?
What if we're all killed by a psychotic fairy?
What if…what if…what if…what if it's amazing and you love it?

You're just being stupid now…

Listen to that one

We all have that voice
The whiny voice that wants to hold you back
The voice, the voice that tells you you shouldn't
The voice that'd make you stay at home every day, under the
duvet so you don't fuck it up
The voice that'll tell you you're comfortable

I mean, it is definitely worth listening to that voice
Very, very occasionally they save you
Either from a probable death experience or even worse, one of
mortifying embarrassment
that'll haunt you until you leave the country

But most times
Kick it's weasley arse out the door
Give it the marital 'yes, dear'
Pat that voice on the head in the most condescending manner
and say 'yes I promise I'll take your view into account'

Then listen to the other voice
The one wearing thigh length Docs, a gold lamè jacket and a
viking hat
The one the tells you that yes you can
The one that told those 50s parent's that they can't put baby in
the corner

That one, listen to that one all the time*

Mostly

Trauma ivy

The very second the event happened
A tiny seed floated unnoticed on the breeze and landed gently
onto my skin
Trauma ivy, implanted
It didn't grow straight away
But as the adrenaline faded, the germination took place

It rooted directly into my soul
Every memory, every trigger, every thought - all fed it's growth

Slowly, tendrils started to spread around my torso
Over the next few years they multiplied and started to cover
more and more of me

Easy to hide for the first few years
But as the new moons continued to pass, the trauma ivy got
more and more difficult to hide

It started to smother all of my existence, as I snapped off one
shoot that peeked out from
behind my defences, another broke my armour elsewhere

And another one

One more

Until

I missed one

Too late, they saw it

Run, avoid them, they saw it, don't let them ask
Change town, change country, change job, change friends,
change faces, change persona, change mask

Another place, another life

The ivy is now entrenched within every crevice of my body

He saw it, I moved
She saw it, I best get a new pair of running shoes, I'm going to
need them

Pick up the rucksack again, I barely unpacked that time

The wriggling, writhing mass of trauma ivy is now suffocating,
rearing it's auxin fuelled tips at a rate I can not keep up with

Stopping any attempt to form a relationship

Until
I've used up all my fight
I've used up all my flight

I give in, it's won
Two choices remain

Both difficult
Both require immense courage

Which one do I pick?

*You didn't need to apologise Stuart, I was hiding it as best as I could

Coerced Dad dancing

No
No
No, I don't want to dance
No, I don't want to shuffle from side to side apathetically with
my arms perched awkwardly in front of me

If U2 from 1983 decided to rerun Redrocks
INXS at Sydney harbour
The Pistols at the 100 club
The Stones on the Isle of Wight in 1970
If I could time travel back to a thousand great concerts
Then I'd dance
I'd be leaping around like an over excited idiot until the sweat
drenched my entire body

Big Country at Liverpool uni in 1986
Fingers at any point over the last 40 years
I'd be the most enthusiastic oaf in the moshpit

But do I want to politely sway whilst tapping heels?
No, not one single bit

Friday night in the Electric Ballroom
Tuesday night in Gossips
Saturday night Slimelight…
Then I danced
I flailed limbs with the best of them
And I'd flail them again if I was there now

Coerced Dad dancing should become a crime
Especially to bland middle-class mediocre music that has haunted
my ears since the 90s
'Dance like nobody is watching?'
If nobody is watching....then I don't have to dance
I call it Schrödinger dancing

*As soon as I know we're going anywhere with a live band, I know how
half of the night is going to go. We can all probably guess most of the play
list, culminating in middle aged bouncing to Mr bloody Brightside and
polite moshing to I bet that you look good on the dance floor...*

Can you have a poo in a unisex loo? (Number 2)

Large shiny glass fronted offices
Automatic rotating door
Only just in time for a meeting
No time to stop before

Welcomed at reception
Shown to a buttonless lift
Really need the toilet
Your bowels begin to shift

One thing is for certain
In an office quite so new
That when you make your excuses
It'll be a unisex loo

"The toilet sir?
Turn right at the corridor."
Then the exhilaration
When you see just a plastic man on the door

*Number one of this poem was written by Paul Edmunds and is much more succinct, it just reads simply, "No"

I sit

I sit
My coffee sits
I'm still sitting

Does everyone have a 'they'?

Everybody has buttons that other people can press
In me there is a fairly well hidden button
One that people seldom find
One labelled 'Fucked off', much harsher than it's freely available relative 'Tetchy'
You can work out what happens when somebody presses it

Most people on this planet don't know where it is
Some do, but choose not to press it

Then…
Then…there is one person
Who doesn't so much as press it
They jump up and down on it
They seem to have access to Thor's hammer and sometimes decide to hit that button as hard and as frequently as they can
They hold it pressed with a force comparable to that inside a singularity, until the hypothetical relaxed horizon feels nothing more than an improbable concept

They will decide how long this period of pressing will be

And then…
And then…**they** say
They say, as though the preceding prolonged period of mental torture never happened…

Dad, can I go to…
Can I have some…
Can I get…
Can I have a new…
Can I…
Can I…
Can I…

Utterly oblivious to the pain, torment, self doubt, anger and melange of other negative emotions that **they** have just put you through

Do you have a **they**?

We both knew

We both knew I wasn't going to win the race to the sea
It wasn't even a contest
It's been a two year changing of the guard
A two year swing in ability
One of growth
The other - decline

I may have mass and experience on my side
But you're gaining on both of those too

It was not the sad nor the bittersweet moment I thought it might
be
As the metaphorical baton invisibly yet inexorably passed
Just a feeling of pride
A feeling that whispered
'Go get 'em son'

My fifteen minutes

I lay on the walls of Jerusalem
A perfect level of warmth emanating from the stones below
Complimented with a gentle cooking from the sun wandering
slowly across the sky

The people around me
The events of the last few days
The wall
The sun
The smells and noises of the old town
All fed a contentedness within me that I'd not felt for what felt
like an eternity

My fifteen minutes was here
My choice to be made

Roll to my left and the floor is 2 foot away
To my right?
A 200 foot drop onto rocks
I could go out on a high from a high

Choose hope for the future
Or accept this moment as the best it is going to get

I hooked my left leg on the side of the wall and anchored my foot
to the floor
Stayed for a while longer, enjoyed the sun and hoped for my
future

Who needs a bear?

We could donate his organs and let someone else live
Perhaps give him science and let him be a cadaver
Alas, there is *one* alternative
One that some may not savour

My Dad you see, is covered in hair
Not on his head, all over his body and back
His coat now shiny like a silverbacks fur
Far from its original black

So rather than the usual burial or cremation
I'll stop them before the fire is lit or grave is dug
He could be a useful decoration
As a beautiful Dad skin rug

We're happy to call…

As a society, there is a skill in which we are great at
We're all quite happy to tell a twat that they are just that

Yet when it comes to those who do good
Do we tell them, no, we don't think we should…

We have many words for that pain the arse
Plenty to choose from, they are definitely not sparse

And yes, we're happy to tell them almost every day
Flick them the V's as their car goes a different way

But when was the last time you just told someone they're great?
No particular reason, maybe not even a mate

Send someone a message, to tell them they made you smile
Even if you haven't spoken to them for quite a while

But no we don't do that, it feels creepy and cheesy
But throwing an insult? That is too easy

Where would I be

Where would I be?
Without my words

Pent up frustrations
Anger burning inside

A scrap of paper
Something with which to scrawl

Then move on with my day
Stresses now cast aside

Without my words
Where would I be?

Acknowledgements

If you have invested your time into reading this, thank you. Time is one of those things we are all short of, and can I be the first to suggest you shouldn't use any of it watching A Question of Sport.